THE PRICE OF A SLICE

Long Vowel Sounds with Consonant Blends

Brian P. Cleary

Illustrations by **Jason Miskimins**

Consultant:
Alice M. Maday
PhD in Early Childhood Education with a Focus in Literacy
Assistant Professor, Retired
Department of Curriculum and Instruction
University of Minnesota

Lerner Publications ◆ Minneapolis

Text copyright © 2022 by Brian P. Cleary
Illustrations copyright © 2022 by Lerner Publishing Group, Inc.

All rights reserved. International copyright secured. No part of this book may be reproduced, stored in a retrieval system, or transmitted in any form or by any means—electronic, mechanical, photocopying, recording, or otherwise—without the prior written permission of Lerner Publishing Group, Inc., except for the inclusion of brief quotations in an acknowledged review.

Lerner Publications Company
An imprint of Lerner Publishing Group, Inc.
241 First Avenue North
Minneapolis, MN 55401 USA

For reading levels and more information, look up this title at www.lernerbooks.com.

Main body text set in Mikado. Typeface provided by HVD.

Library of Congress Cataloging-in-Publication Data

Names: Cleary, Brian P., 1959- author. | Miskimins, Jason, illustrator. | Maday, Alice M., consultant.
Title: The price of a slice : long vowel sounds with consonant blends / Brian P. Cleary ; illustrations by Jason Miskimins ; consultant: Alice M. Maday.
Description: Minneapolis : Lerner Publications , [2022] | Series: Phonics fun | Audience: Ages 4-8. | Audience: Grades K-1. | Summary: "The swine put twine on my spine. With rhyming, carefully leveled text and comedic, colorful illustrations, this book provides plenty of examples of long vowel sounds with consonant blends and encourages readers to try the sounds for themselves"— Provided by publisher.
Identifiers: LCCN 2021032419 (print) | LCCN 2021032420 (ebook) | ISBN 9781728441283 (library binding) | ISBN 9781728448510 (paperback) | ISBN 9781728444895 (ebook)
Subjects: LCSH: English language—Vowels—Juvenile literature. | English language—Consonants—Juvenile literature. | English language—Phonetics—Juvenile literature. | Reading—Phonetic method—Juvenile literature.
Classification: LCC PE1157 .C557 2022 (print) | LCC PE1157 (ebook) | DDC 428.1/3—dc23

LC record available at https://lccn.loc.gov/2021032419
LC ebook record available at https://lccn.loc.gov/2021032420

Manufactured in the United States of America
3-53630-49742-7/8/2022

Dear Parents and Educators,

As a former adult literacy coach and the father of three children, I know that learning to read isn't always easy. That's why I developed **Phonics Fun**—a series that employs a combination of devices to help children learn to read. This book uses rhyme, repetition, illustration, and phonics to introduce young readers to long vowel sounds and consonant blends—"sound-outable" letter combinations such as *fl*, *tr*, *br*, and *st*.

The bridge to literacy is one of the most important we will ever cross. It's my hope that the Phonics Fun series will help new readers to hop, gallop, and skip from one side to the other!

Sincerely,

Brian P. Cleary

Note to Readers

This book is all about long vowel sounds and consonant blends. You can hear them in words like **sleep** and **snake**. The **bold** words in this book have long vowel sounds and consonant blends. They also rhyme!

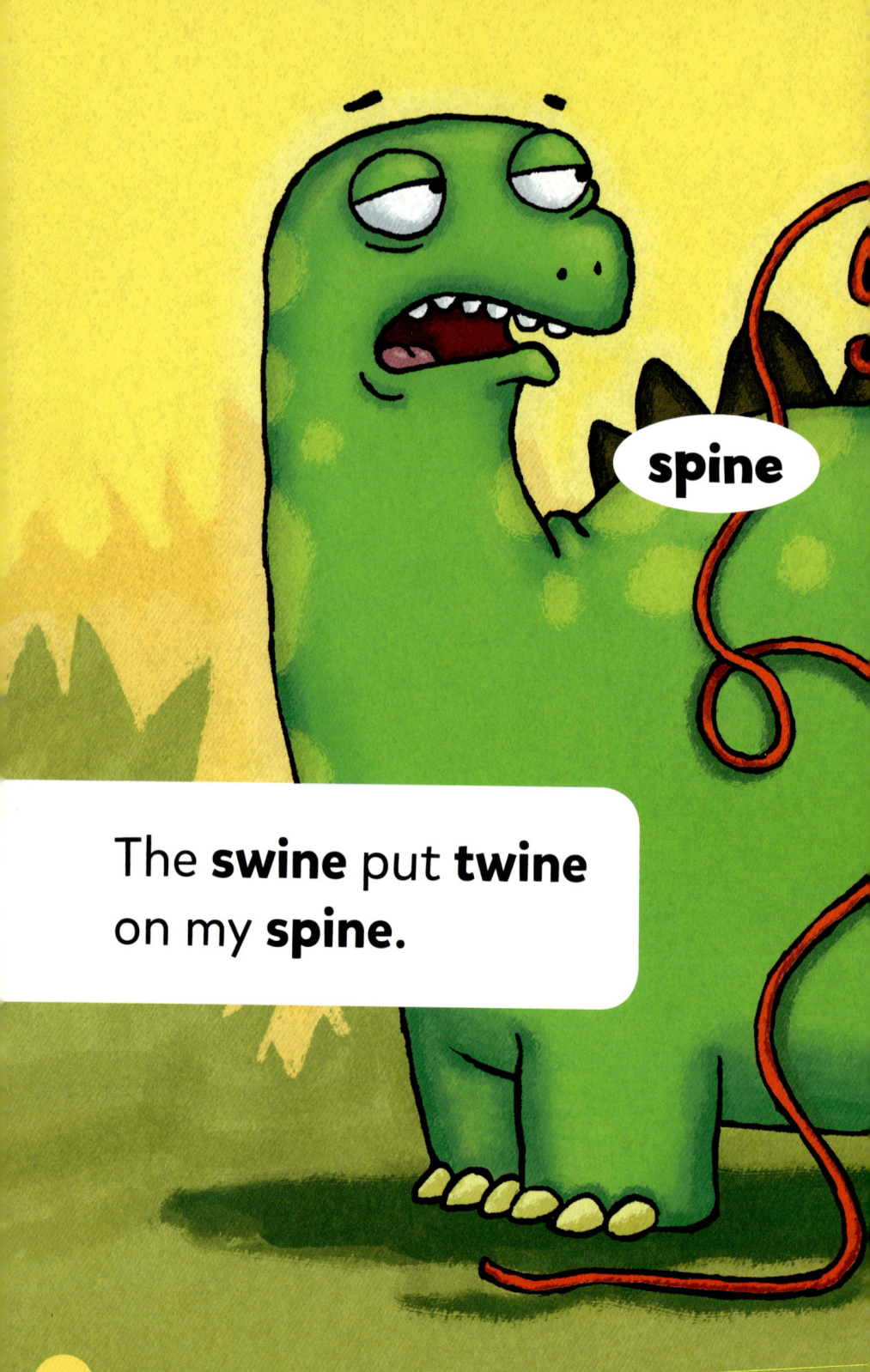

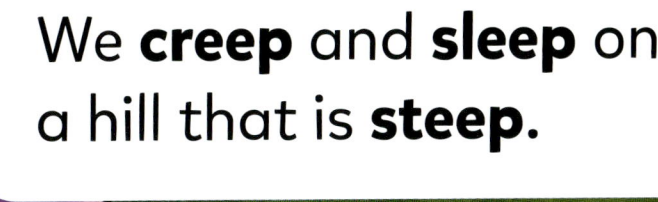

We **creep** and **sleep** on a hill that is **steep**.

The **steam** came from the **cream** in a **dream**.

I **cry** when I **try** to **fly** in the **sky**.

The **fleet** can meet and **greet** in the **sleet**.

It is **true** that he **drew** with **blue glue.**

Blake and the **snake** ate a **steak** by the lake.

The mice paid **twice** the **price** for the **spice** and the **slice**.

Make Your Own

Use the words on these pages to write a story with long vowel sounds and consonant blends!

swine **sleep**

fly **glue**

tree **snake**